ChordTime® Piano

Hits

Level 2B

I-IV-V⁷ chords
in C, G and F

This book belongs to: _____

Arranged by

Randall Faber and Jon Ophoff

Special Thanks to Christopher Oill
Editor: Isabel Otero Bowen
Design and Illustration: Terpstra Design, San Francisco
Engraving: Dovetree Productions, Inc.

FABER

PIANO ADVENTURES®

3042 Creek Drive
Ann Arbor, Michigan 48108

A NOTE TO TEACHERS

ChordTime® Piano Hits is an outstanding collection of popular songs arranged for the Level 2B pianist. Enjoy blockbusters, chart-toppers, and award-winners as performed by stars such as Ed Sheeran, Meghan Trainor, Imagine Dragons, and more.

Not only is **ChordTime Piano Hits** appealing to the student, it is especially formulated for the piano teacher! In keeping with the "ChordTime" concept, the songs are arranged to provide the student opportunity for chord recognition and chord practice, particularly of the I, IV, and V chords. The keys are limited to C, G, and F, with warm-up exercises for each key.

ChordTime Piano Hits is part of the *ChordTime Piano* series. "ChordTime" designates Level 2B of the *PreTime®* to *BigTime® Piano Supplementary Library* arranged by Faber and Faber.

Following are the levels of the supplementary library, which lead from *PreTime to BigTime*.

PreTime® Piano	(Primer Level)
PlayTime® Piano	(Level 1)
ShowTime® Piano	(Level 2A)
ChordTime® Piano	(Level 2B)
FunTime® Piano	(Level 3A – 3B)
BigTime® Piano	(Level 4)

Each level offers books in a variety of styles, making it possible for the teacher to offer stimulating material for every student. For a complimentary detailed listing, e-mail faber@pianoadventures.com or write us at the mailing address below.

Visit us at **PianoAdventures.com**.

Helpful Hints:

1. This book presents the I, IV, V, and vi chords in the keys of C, G, and F. The vi chord is included because of its prevalence in current pop music.

2. The chord warm-ups for a given key should be played daily before practicing the songs. Try to identify the I, IV, V, and vi chords in each song, writing chord symbols below the bass staff.

3. The warm-ups highlight common chord progressions. Can you find recurring chord progressions in the songs?

4. The warm-ups progress in difficulty. Transpose the later warm-ups to all three keys: C major, G major, and F major.

5. For further review of I, IV, and V chords, use additional ChordTime books.

6. For next steps with the vi chord, use Piano Adventures® Levels 3A and 3B in combination with Piano Adventures Scale and Chord Book 2.

ISBN 978-1-61677-718-0

TABLE OF CONTENTS

Key of C

Practice these warm-ups before playing songs in the key of C.
The **I**, **IV**, and **V** chords are called the *primary* chords, built on steps 1, 4, and 5 of the major scale.

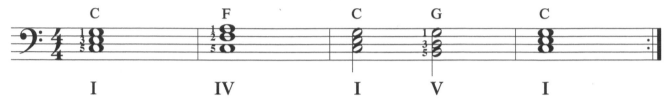

The **vi** chord, built on scale step 6, is also common in popular chord progressions.
Whereas the I, IV, and V chords are major, the vi chord is minor.

The Middle

**Words and Music by SARAH AARONS, MARCUS LOMAX,
JORDAN JOHNSON, ANTON ZASLAVSKI, KYLE TREWARTHA,
MICHAEL TREWARTHA and STEFAN JOHNSON**

Driving (♩ = 100–108)

6

Brave

Words and Music by SARA BAREILLES
and JACK ANTONOFF

FF3051

out. Hon - est - ly, I wan - na

see you be brave. I just wan - na see you, I____

____ just wan - na see you, I____ just wan - na

see you,____ I wan - na see you be brave.

Meant to Be

Words and Music by BLETA REXHA, JOSH MILLER,
TYLER HUBBARD and DAVID GARCIA

FF3051

Key of G

Practice these warm-ups before playing songs in the key of G.
The **I**, **IV**, and **V** chords are called the *primary* chords, built on steps 1, 4, and 5 of the major scale.

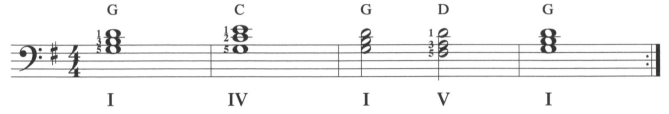

The **vi** chord, built on scale step 6, is also common. Memorize these two popular chord progressions.

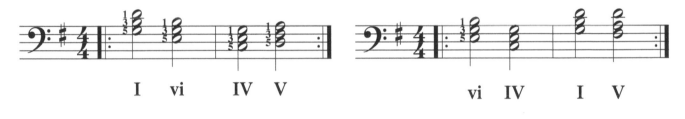

Perfect

Words and Music by
ED SHEERAN

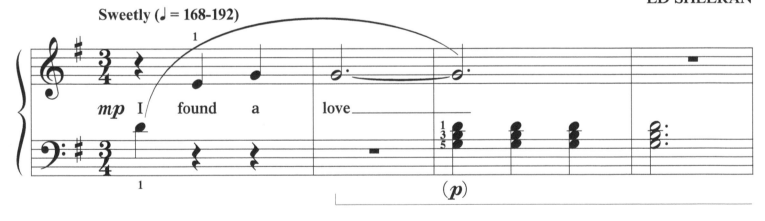

grass, lis - ten - ing to our fav' - rite song.

When you said you looked a mess, I whis - pered

prepare

un - der - neath my breath, but you heard it, "Dar - ling,

you look per - fect to - night."

rit.

p

from *Zootopia*

Try Everything

Words and Music by SIA FURLER,
TOR ERIK HERMANSEN and MIKKEL ERIKSEN

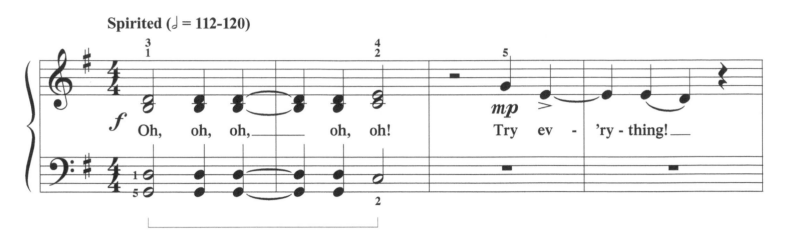

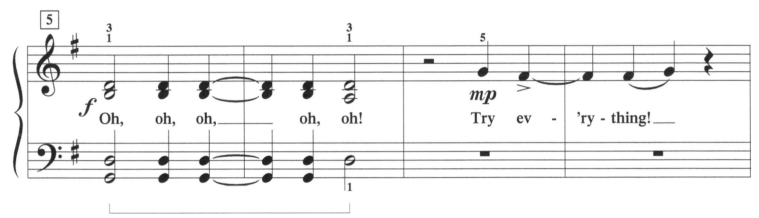

16

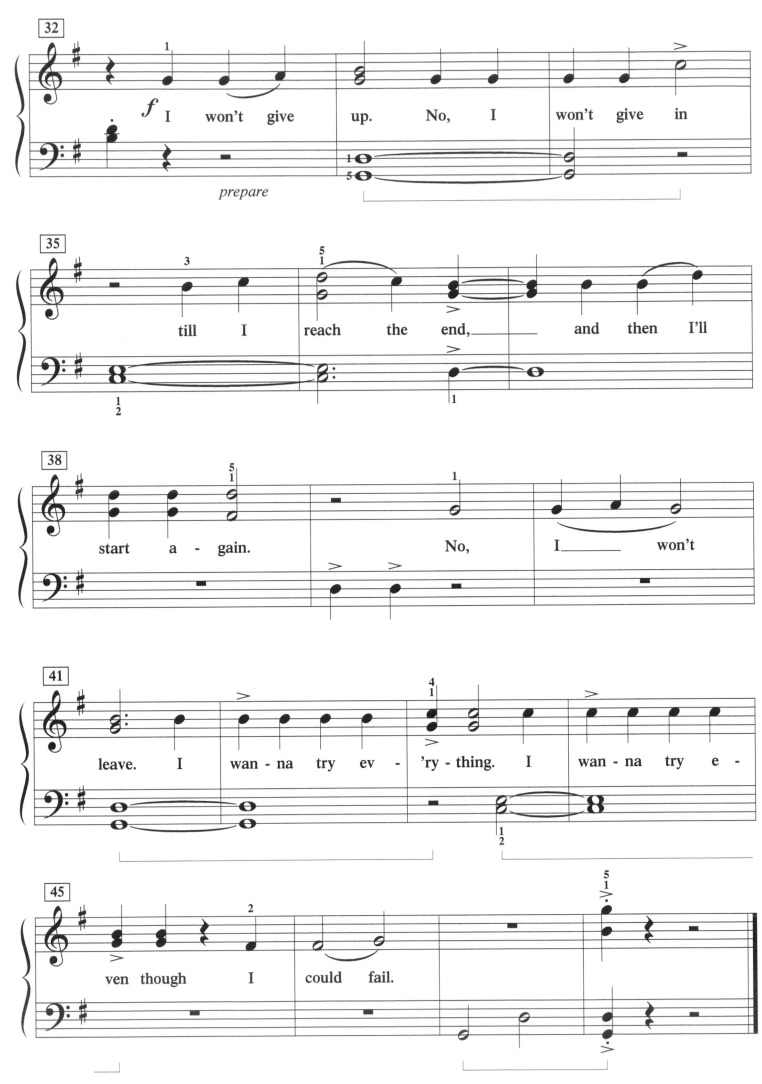

from *The Greatest Showman*

This Is Me

Words and Music by BENJ PASEK
and JUSTIN PAUL

FF3051

Thunder

Words and Music by DAN REYNOLDS, WAYNE SERMON,
BEN MCKEE, DANIEL PLATZMAN, ALEXANDER GRANT
and JAYSON DEZUZIO

Key of F

Practice these warm-ups before playing songs in the key of F.
The **I**, **IV**, and **V** chords are called the *primary* chords, built on steps 1, 4, and 5 of the major scale.

The **iii** chord and **vi** chord, built on scale steps 3 and 6, are also common in popular progressions.
Whereas the I, IV, and V chords are major, the iii and vi chords are minor.

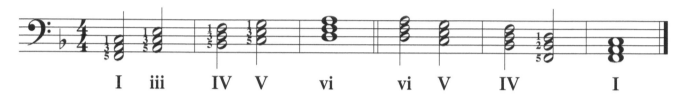

Rather Be

Words and Music by GRACE CHATTO,
JACK PATTERSON, NICOLE MARSHALL
and JAMES NAPIER

Swift and light (♩ = 100-116)

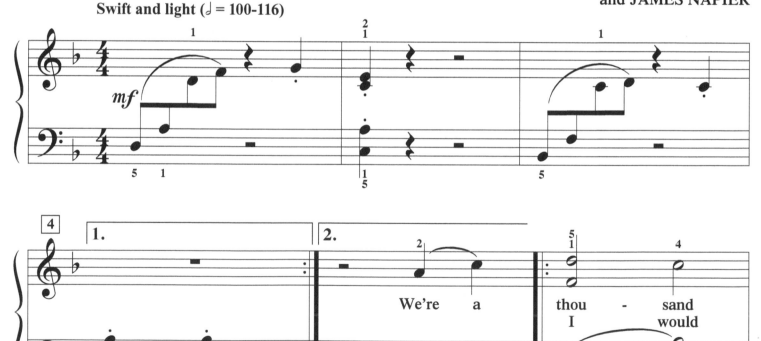

24

Like I'm Gonna Lose You

Words and Music by CAITLYN ELIZABETH SMITH,
JUSTIN WEAVER and MEGHAN TRAINOR

High Hopes

Words and Music by BRENDON URIE, SAMUEL HOLLANDER,
WILLIAM LOBBAN BEAN, JONAS JEBERG, JACOB SINCLAIR,
JENNY OWEN YOUNGS, ILSEY JUBER, LAUREN PRITCHARD and TAYLOR PARKS

Fast and rhythmic (♩ = 144-160)

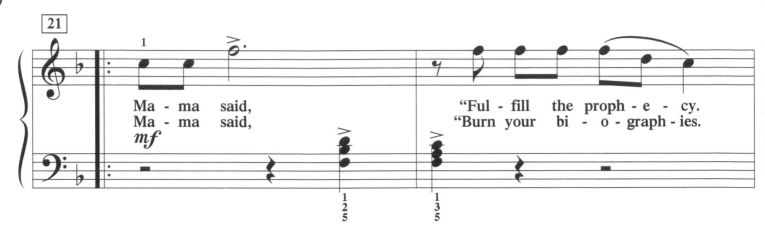

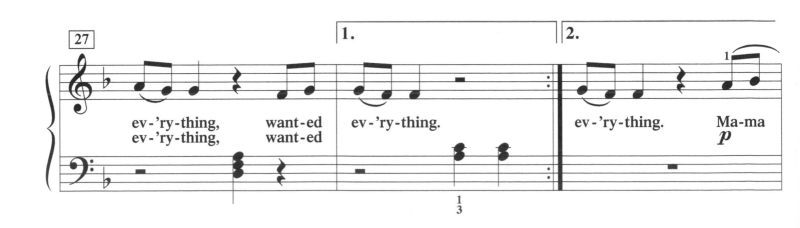

MUSIC DICTIONARY

p	*mp*	*mf*	*f*
piano	*mezzo piano*	*mezzo forte*	*forte*
soft	medium soft	medium loud	loud

crescendo (cresc.)
Play gradually louder.

diminuendo (dim.) or decrescendo (decresc.)
Play gradually softer.

SIGN	TERM	DEFINITION
	a tempo	Return to the original tempo.
	accent	Play this note louder.
	chord progression	A recurring series of chords.
D.S. al Fine	*Dal Segno al Fine*	Return to the 𝄋 sign and play until the *Fine* (end).
	fermata	Hold this note longer than usual.
	Fine	End here.
1. 2.	**1st and 2nd endings**	Play the 1st ending and take the repeat. Then play the 2nd ending, skipping over the 1st ending.
or	**key signature**	The key signature indicates the sharps or flats to be played for the key of the piece (major or minor). It is written at the beginning of each line of music.
8*va* – ¬	*ottava*	Play one octave higher than written. When 8*va* – ⌐ is below the staff, play one octave lower.
⌐∧⌐	**pedal change**	Lift the damper pedal as the note is played. Depress the pedal immediately after.
⌐_⌐	**pedal mark**	Depress the damper pedal (right-foot pedal) after the note or chord.
4/4 ♩ ♩ ♩ ♩	**pick-up note (upbeat)**	An incomplete first measure. A pick-up note(s) leads to the first full measure. Often the last measure will also be incomplete. Then, the combined value of the first and last measure equals one complete measure.
	The primary (main) chords	These are the names for the three most common chords in any key: **I** is the Roman numeral for 1. **IV** is the Roman numeral for 4. **V** is the Roman numeral for 5.
rit.	*ritardando (ritard.)*	Gradually slow down.
	scale	The word scale comes from the Latin word for "ladder." The notes of a scale move up or down by 2nds. All seven letters of the musical alphabet are used in a major scale. Ex. C-D-E-F-G-A-B-C
	slur	Connect the notes within a slur.
	staccato	Play *staccato* notes detached, disconnected.
	tempo	The speed of music.
4/4, 3/4, 2/4	**time signature**	Two numbers at the beginning of a piece (one above the other). The top number indicates the number of beats per measure; the bottom number indicates the note receiving the beat.